Dancing in The Sun
FINDING JOY IN THE MOMENT

IMELDA SAMANIEGO

DANCING IN THE SUN: FINDING JOY IN THE MOMENT
Copyright © 2022 **Imelda Samaniego**

All rights reserved. No part of this book may be used or reproduced by any means, graphic, electronic, or mechanical, including photocopying, recording, taping or by information storage and retrieval system without the written permission of the author except in the case of brief quotations embodied in critical articles and reviews.

Stratton Press Publishing
831 N Tatnall Street Suite M #188,
Wilmington, DE 19801
www.stratton-press.com
1-888-323-7009

Because of the dynamic nature of the Internet, any web addresses or links contained in this book may have changed since publication and may no longer be valid. The views expressed in the work are solely those of the author and do not necessarily reflect the views of the publisher, and the publisher hereby disclaims any responsibility for them.

ISBN (Paperback): 979-8-88764-229-1
ISBN (Hardback): 979-8-88764-230-7
ISBN (Ebook): 979-8-88764-231-4

Printed in the United States of America

This book is dedicated to hope. Despite hardships and heartache, one must keep finding some happiness in unfortunate circumstances. No matter how much pain one experiences, remembering better times can lift spirits. J. M. Barrie said it best: "God gave us memories so we may have roses in December." Create bliss within the present moment as it cultivates joy for tomorrow. Always remember to dance in the sun.

Let us be grateful to the people who make us happy;
They are the charming gardeners who make our souls blossom.

— Marcel Proust

Thank you for believing in me and nuturing my broken spirit with constant support

~ Imelda

Contents

Poetry ix

    Relentless 1
    Quaking Soul 2
    Secret Regret 3
    Every Day 4
    Crumpled Flower 5
    Cyanide Upon My Tongue 6
    Into Eternity 7
    Stepping into Your Sun 8
    Returning Footsteps 9
    The Wait 11
    Immortal Love 12
    No Restraint 13

Short Fiction 15

    The River of Life 17
    The Broken Heart 21
    University Frolics 25
    Furry Mutiny 29
    Feline Doppler Effect 34
    Possum Race 39

About the Author 43

Poetry

Relentless

There is a need for warmth
It is cold, dark, and rainy outside as well as within in my soul
Inside I weep with silent screams
He finds his way in

He looms forth in my brain torturing me with memories of yesterday
When times were beautiful and the relationship young
Even those moments he cut me down to my bare bone
The pain seems to grip my heart and not let go

My heart cares for him still despite the harm done
Mind chastises in an exercise of mere futility
Emotions have the upper hand
A love so relentless it endures the test of time

Quaking Soul

Rooms whisper late in the evening
Of times when laughter and soft kisses reigned
Windows reflect happiness they once witnessed
Soft sheets rustle out their recorded history of romance long since gone

Dust has gathered in the quiet moments
Lives have parted leaving behind only memories
The strong mind may have made an effort to move on
Only that soft gentle heart remains in a forgotten corner of time

Yet in the center of that ruined past is a lit candle
Flickering flame of hope dances on the wick
Love remains alive
Beating loudly enough to bring that quaking soul to its knees

Secret Regret

In the dusty corner of your past I sit
Mourning your absence in darkness
Tears bathing my cheeks in sorrow deep
Heart beating out hope of your return

Forevermore your girl
Holding onto dreams
Despite the vicelike grip of pain
Loving the tenderness of what once was

Your deeds and words blaze themselves upon my mind
My soul will never forget our dance in the sun
So I remain in my place
Quietly waiting in the ashes of your secret regret

Every Day

Anything from him lit my world
His infectious smile
Laughter from that barrel of a chest
The trailing touch from his wide hand across my lower back

Contact in electronic form
A knock on my door
The ring of my cell phone
That soft sigh during an embrace

With every sunrise, he comes to my mind
In each sunset, I lie down to dream of him
My universe revolved for him and him alone
He always resides in my heart at the beginning and end of every day

Crumpled Flower

My well is dry
The source is tapped
At your leisure and pleasure
With my blind permission

Love's rose-colored glasses hinder sight
In utter devotion, I gave again and again
Life's blood spilled in your name
A heart upon the altar in sacrifice to your demands

I gave you my all
Until I was a husk of my former self
Now you move on
Leaving the crumpled flower on the floor

Cyanide Upon My Tongue

My double-edged sword
Whom I willingly plunge into my beating heart again and again
The one who heals and wounds
Weapon of my choosing and demise of my soul

Producer of cries both in pleasure and pain
Strong hands that torture me with delight so rare
Sweet voice that serenades and whips ferociously
Arms that embrace my weeping self after the damage has been done

Treacherous love
Rare and divine
The loaded vial of poison that I crave
Cyanide upon my tongue

Into Eternity

There's a slow death
Torture with a delicate touch
Watching the light of your life sink below the horizon
Leaving your world in a tender sunset

Savoring the silky whispers of skin against skin
Treasuring the traveling lips
Clasped strong hands
Desperate kisses

The heart renders in two
Separation looms ahead
Eyelashes wet with tears
Prayers uttered

The soul pleads for a miracle
Let us beat the odds
Deliver us from the melting despair
Preserve the love we have into eternity

Stepping into Your Sun

You are that voice in the darkness silencing my inner demons
Taming inner wild spirits bucking sensibilities

A balm to my war-torn heart
The taste of peace in chaos

Healing feather light touch
Mesmerizing scent of skin

A sun-dappled summer afternoon
Refreshing breeze in stifling heat

Serenade of rain on terracotta tiles
Cold water upon the parched tongue

Lit candle dispelling darkness
Casting shadows aside, I step into your sun

Returning Footsteps

My heart aches
A part of me is missing

You are my great passion,
My great love

How clearly you appear in my dreams,
You are in my blood, my soul

I cry out your name to the endless sky,
Summoning the spirits to assist me

An inner voice whispers your name,
Visions of your face appear everywhere

The time has come to open your eyes,
To see the wondrous life that awaits us

Open your heart,
Allow my love to penetrate the barriers

Fly quickly to me,
Fall into my loving arms

Does your heart not ache,
When you are alone in your thoughts—thinking of me

Do you not yearn
For my gentle ways, my loving spirit

Shed the negative thoughts,
That bend your mind

Come back to my warm embrace,
Come bask in the warmth of my unconditional love

And I shall always be grateful,
When I hear your footsteps outside the door

Returning to me

The Wait

I am haunted
Restless mind keeps racing
Worries bubble over
Waiting for the call

Done all I could
Pressed him close with kisses
Listened to the sorrow in his voice
Loved in silence

Released him to the south wind
No tethers or tracking monitors
Just enough trust
Plenty of love

Bowing my dark head in prayer
Eyes closed with fluttering eyelashes
Lips slightly moving with the words for God
Divine assistance invoked

Comfort him
Give him the strength of a rock
Let him feel Thy enveloping embrace
Protect him until he is home again

Bring him back to me
Into my arms
Wrapped up in my heart
Tell him I wait with patience and endless love

Immortal Love

Long after I have gone
My body returned back to the earth
It will be my love story for you which will live on
With strength and power that can never die

A tale that will transcend space and time
Speak to the future generations
Of dedication, loyalty, and fierce passion
It will teach lessons of life and how to endure the pain of loss

My heart and soul will become infused in ink
Wet hot tears seal the saga deep into paper
Memory and love are immortal
Thus the world will forever know of my feelings for you

No Restraint

Winds blow and change the course of life
Everything is in the hands of fate
Nothing is ever certain
Only love

Live in the moment of the sun
When all you know is happiness
In the arms of your beloved
Feeling your hearts beat as one

It can be taken in a blink of the eye
In your darkness that memory draws light
At least you knew life
Felt alive and soared into the blue

Treasure the time you have now
Lean into that embrace a little harder
Kiss deeper
Love with no restraint

Short Fiction

The River of Life

The sun shone like a sphere of iridescent gold hung against the azure skies nestled among the feathery clouds. Sounds of the river lapped on the rocky banks in the distance, and the gulls cawed overhead. On a glorious day, my beloved mariner was laid to rest by his favorite body of water. Leaning against a tree with my feet buried deep in the grass, I sighed looking over the funeral from several yards away. My dark curls flapped in the wind like sails, and tears glittered on my eyelashes like jewels. The heart that beat within my breast was bleeding in sorrow and my soul rent in two. I was not even permitted to toss a rose upon the casket by the family much less attend the graveside service. So I stood off on a nearby hill and waited my turn to pay respect in the silence.

Once the grieving entourage had left the grave site, I made my way down the grassy slopes. The tombstone was a lovely dark blue marble with gold etched words. Smiling softly, I gently traced his name with my fingers. Sinking into the fresh dirt upon my knees, I fell against the cold stone, watering the earth with my tears. Pressing my lips to a simple mariner's cross around my neck, I whispered his name. Slowly I took off the pendant and lay it down at the foot of the tombstone. We always would have the days spent together on the river behind the helm basking in God's blessings.

"Who were you to him?" a quiet baritone voice startled me with the inquiry. I whipped around to see one of the sons step out from behind a monument and walk toward me.

"Mother only called you a whore and holds such animosity toward you. Pitted everyone against you on an accusation that probably holds no merit." The teen came to stand by his father's headstone and gazed curiously at my tears. "You truly feel his loss as strongly as we do. I think you meant something to Dad too. We found this knitted washcloth doused in rose perfume folded neatly beneath his pillow. Not any work done by Mother or my sisters nor did the scent belong to them either. Other things were found as well, but none as delicate as the cloth. I wanted to meet you and know who you were to my dad." The boy squatted down before me and tilted my head up to look directly in my eyes.

"I loved him with a depth of the ocean and a loyalty as fierce as a bloodhound," I uttered through the rising sobs. My beloved's son nodded and squeezed my shoulder, pressing me to calm down. Wiping my tears, I steadied myself. "We kept company for so many years and only recently did we express romantic love. He taught me how to live again. My soul danced, and there was light in my eyes once again. The joy your father gave me was a rare treasure never to be had before or after. I stood by his side in love and support through his tempest and on the sunny days as well. Though he may never had loved me the way I did him, it never mattered. As long as I was blessed by his company, I knew God in our relationship. Your father was my gift, and I tended to him as such. Always remember him as the man who stood strong as an aged cracked rock, which was the stone fortress against life's storms."

"You were the one he smelled of when he came to visit us. The one he would go back to again and again. Dad didn't love Mother anymore, and we all knew that. These past few months he came to us happier, and whenever a certain text came through, his face lit up. You were the reason behind his smile and laughter. Dad may have been the cathedral and castle for us all, but you were his flying buttress." The wisdom far exceeded the young man's years as they rolled off his tongue. Blushing, I looked down in embarrassment at the compliment. My man's son kissed the top of my head as gently as his father had done so many times. "Thank you for loving Dad and being a part of his happiness." With the gratitude expressed, the teen left me to my grieving.

"You did right by that son," I whispered to the grave, patting the dirt. Stroking the face of the tombstone, smiling, I uttered, "He will grow up to be a fine man who knows where true value lies—the heart." Crying, I kissed the glittering letters one last time in a somber farewell. "Though you may be gone, your love will remain ever present and transcend time through those whom you held close. I'll always love you." I walked away from the cemetery, dragging my feet along with a heavy heart, but with the knowledge I had at least loved and was loved on the river of life.

The Broken Heart

The heat pulsated in the humid air slowing every living thing down. Allison waited in the parking lot feeling the hot pavement radiate fire through her thin ballet shoes. Twisting her hands nervously, she kept scanning the train platform for sight of her man. Too many days had passed since Allison spoke or seen Joe last, and he was finally coming home.

As to the capacity Joe was going to hold in Allison's life, it was uncertain. To her aching heart, he would always be the only one who breathed life back into her dead soul. Now things had changed in his absence, and Allison felt it deep inside. Being the other woman is never easy, and nobody ever sees her personal torment. Only the one who bore his ring and yet never had his heart, only obligation, had the compassion of others. What of the other woman? She loves the man too and with more ferocity no doubt. Yet her chance and risk of losing him was greater due to an institution of duty. What of the happiness between the man and that lady who wore the scarlet letter upon her breast? Allison loved despite the taboo, jeers, sneers, and glares of others. To her, all that mattered was how Joe loved her and had her spirit dance a dervish. The light shone in her eyes again and she lived. The uncertainty of the longevity of the relationship Allison had with him would always weigh heavy on her mind. After all, she was working with borrowed time, and she had cast the dice with her heart in the gamble.

The train rolled into the station through a massive cloud of smoke. Finally emerging from the industrial mess was Joe's tall sturdy form walking toward the lot. His auburn hair was lit by the sun and those sea glass eyes shone bright as he looked for the one who always waited. Allison ran toward him, her dark hair flowing behind her in a black sail flapping in her wake, flinging herself against him in a desperate embrace. "I missed you!"

Joe staggered back, nearly knocked down by the passionate love expressed. "Missed you too, Ally," a husky whisper replied as he buried his face in Allison's neck, taking in her scent. They held each other in that insane summer day not caring of the inquisitive yes of the crowd that milled about them. Only aware of the reunion and the undying love Allison had for Joe.

Allison drove Joe to his house, listening to him prattle on about his children and the wife. "The kids are doing great! Fanny finally got her LCSW and will have a clinic waiting for her to join them in a few weeks. Mind you, she has to move out of the house for all this. Everyone will be so delighted. Paul graduated from the university and finally has that PhD in history. Several job offers from all prominent colleges are just pouring in! That boy is going to go so far in this life. Might even take after my father and become a noted historian! Tim is still struggling a lot with drugs. We got him into a good rehab center in the next state over. Time will tell with that one. Beth is doing great as docent at the museum and even is one over the weekends at the cathedral in town. Takes after my side of the family no doubt." Laughter filled his voice, and pride puffed his chest up.

Joe's bloodline had ties to the colonial backbone of the country thus his seed proved to be exceptional. If he had gotten anything right in life, it was producing four wonderful people who would contribute much to society. There was no doubt Joe lived for his offspring—every dime he earned was poured into them. Allison squeezed his hand, sharing his joy, and he looked her way with affection.

They arrived at Joe's house and Allison put the car into park. The dreaded words came from those gentle lips. "I have decided something, Ally. It is very hard to say this, but you know how much I love my kids. If the right job is offered in my hometown, I am going to take it. I am leaving you, Ally."

"Oh god." Allison's heart screamed at the piercing wound, and her soul rent in two. She bent her head down to Joe's lap and pressed her lips to his hand. "You do what you have to do for them." Tears saturated Allison's cheeks, and she rested on Joe's lap spent in body-quaking sobs. She understood the why, but her heart still was in agony.

Joe stroked Allison's hair with care. Leaning back against the car seat, he sighed. This was hard for Joe too for he led two lives and had two sets of hearts who loved him. "Goodbye, sweet Ally." Joe placed Allison back in her place, gathered his things, and went into the house.

The cry that emitted from her lips resounded in the area for miles. It was the sound of the broken heart that many have known intimately themselves. Allison barely made it to her own home, crawling toward the bed with a cut to the quick of her soul. Lying in the place where love was made and her happiness had lived, she watered the mattress and covers in her grief. The sun would no longer shine nor would Allison's heart beat again to the tune of that wondrous love. Her life had ceased and she knew it.

"I can't do this anymore." Allison carefully took a knife from beneath her pillow and stroked its side. She had set the paperwork in order and had left everything to him—the house, money, and the cats. "What reasons have I to live? He's gone. I have done everything noteworthy. I have nothing." Allison inserted the tip of the blade with deliberation and in came down inside with a smooth stroke, severing the arteries beyond repair. Allison had her arms rest into a bucket on either side of the bed for easy clean up. The legal documents lay her bed and the note to the only man whom she ever really loved. It was Allison's time to depart this world, and she gladly went with her heart.

University Frolics

It was a warm spring night on the college campus where my best friend Keith and I worked as security guards. Any notion of peacekeeping or ensuring safety in our job description was nothing more than a joke. Mostly reigning in drunk twenty-something-year-olds was what we did. Zero parental supervision made these kids lose inhibitions. Tonight would be no different as our commanding officer alerted us to another student under the influence needed solitary confinement in campus nurse's station.

Keith groaned as he tossed me our patrol car keys as we headed to it. "What do you think we are going to find, Darren? Drunk or high?" he asked as I drove us toward the now shuttered sports equipment shed. Keith laughed after seeing my eyes roll in his direction. "Right. Doesn't really matter. We still must get that bastard under control. Alright, we do what we always do. I chase him then you cut him off the pass."

Upon our arrival, we found a young man hollering about how hot he was while stripping down to his birthday suit. I can't stand restraining a naked man much less one who had taken psychedelic drugs. Checking to see if both nightstick and pepper spray were readily available on my utility belt, I motioned Keith to start corralling our student along onc side of the building.

Sure enough, that kid ran like his hair was on fire when I shined my flashlight on him while asking if he was okay. Keith followed my direction by chasing him while I waited around the corner for them.

My billy club did a great job at clotheslining that bastard, but he still was junk side up. "On your stomach, kid!" I barked then started nudging his ribs with a toe. That bastard had the audacity to kick at me, which really got my blood pressure sky high. "You asked for it, mister!" I pepper-sprayed his manhood pretty good, sending him howling onto his belly while holding those flaming marbles. No mercy was given as the student got himself some flex cuffs put on. "Yours!" I laughed while shoving that bastard at Keith after hauling him onto his feet.

Once inside the patrol car, Keith started complaining about events that were going to unfold. "Damn it, Darren! I am going to have to help that nurse get this kid hosed off and into some scrubs now. Why did you spice up them nuts? The face is good enough. Crap!" he growled at me from his passenger seat. Keith always hated cleaning my messes but knew he would never do restraint methods as well as I did. Sure enough, everything unfolded at the campus clinic exactly like my buddy predicted.

Nurse Jenny groaned when she saw Keith and I walk through her office doorway with our catch. "High as a kite," she muttered as she shined a light into the kid's steady dilated pupils. When asked if he had consumed mushrooms, that student nodded, grinning like an idiot. Nurse Jenny noticed her patient's red irritated crotch and started to chastise us. "You boys know better than to mace these strung-out morons in their gonads! I need help with this kid in the shower. We have donated jeans he can wear afterwards. Let's get this crap show started!" She motioned at my friend toward a spare medical smock hanging on her office wall coat hook.

While Keith was busy washing our latest donation to Nurse Jenny, I called his girlfriend. "Lana, think you can come over to the college security guard parking lot for your boyfriend's break time? We just had a rough case, and he needs some loving." I asked her using my pleading-voice tone. Per usual, she was game.

Lana greeted Keith and I at the designated spot. My buddy grinned at me as we pulled up to his girlfriend. "Don't say I never did you any favors. Thirty minutes. Just clean up the back seat when you are done." I tossed a Clorox wipes canister at Keith before leaving him to Lana for downtime.

College security guard was no glamorous job, but it can have some perks. Especially if you are my partner and have to handle not so fun duties. I can make being the nurse's assistant worthwhile. After all, university frolics have a possibility of getting enjoyed by everyone from students to security guards.

Furry Mutiny

Petra tucked her dark hair behind her ear and adjusted her coat to fit more snugly around her as the cruel November wind nearly blew her across the road. She took out some gloves from her pockets and blew off the fur, which was evidence of her trade as a pet sitter. Sliding her hands in the warm woolen mittens, Petra smiled and continued her walk to the house where she was staying caring for a menagerie of animals. Under her watch were two dogs, two cats, a bearded dragon, a turtle, and multiple fish. Oh the things one does to stretch fifteen cents into a dollar.

When Petra got to the house, she came upon the pizza delivery man waiting at the door. She had called for the delivery on her cell phone from the car hoping to come home to a hot meal. Once the man had been paid, Petra shuffled into the house and placed the box on the table. Turning around, she examined the contents of the terrarium to ensure Phineas the baby bearded dragon was still in his corner with his roommate Shelly the turtle. Both occupants were dozing off in their remote bedding piles of shaved cedar and bark. Petra turned around and found Honey the red Persian sitting on the table with the aquarium watching the lizard with malicious intent in her dark amber eyes. Sugar the blue point Siamese-Himalayan mix was up on the cat tree surveying the fish and terrarium residents.

"Not on your furry nine lives, babe." Petra stroked Honey and kissed her on the head with affection. Sugar mewed softly, giving her comment to the conversation at which the dark-haired pet sitter blew a kiss at the Himalayan.

Petra shuffled off and began the descent to the basement where the French bull dogs were crated. Fiona the dark-faced female jumped out of the crate and proceeded to claw her way up the girl's dress while her lighter brother Louis padded his way up the stairs in hope for grub. Petra shushed Fiona down and guided her to join the rest of the rabble on the middle floor.

Upon opening the pizza box, the girl was mystified by the raw dough and toppings. "What on God's green earth?" Petra started to read the baking instructions which now had the design of kitty teeth marks on the corners. "Honey!" the pet sitter sighed and then slid the raw pizza in the oven under the supervision of a curious red tabby Persian. "Okay, fluffy munchkin, you and I need some cuddling time." Petra picked up her feline charge and sat on the couch where she proceeded to brush the long fur.

Suddenly, there was voluminous smoke coming from the kitchen soon filling the whole floor. Petra ran to the oven where she discovered that years of lack of use created a film that turned into black smoke when the heat reached a certain temperature. She quickly moved the pizza out and turned on the exhaust fan. With great dismay, Petra found that the blades of the fan moved at a snail's pace proving ineffective. Quickly, she opened the back door and started to move the smoke out by waving a dish rag in the air.

Petra was trying to ensure all feline and canine residents remained inside the house whilst she attempted to vent the home out. Suddenly, a loud bang came from the basement, which caused the girl to jump high. Scurrying madly downstairs, Petra found Fiona had slammed the door to the litter pan room behind her. Sitting there with a cat turn dangling from her mouth, the female dog nearly gave a sheepish grin at the flabbergasted pet sitter. "Fiona, nasty does not even begin to describe your manners," Petra groaned and took the dog by the collar and yanked her up the stairs.

Then the sight of Louis the male French bull dog chomping on a pen greeted the girl in the living room. Black ink was oozing from the sides of his mouth and shards of plastic decorated the circumference of his body. "You are coming with me, mister."

Petra hauled her naughty ward out in the yard. Placing the squirming dog between her knees, the girl took the garden hose and washed his face and mouth. Then using the mustard from the grill ledge, Petra squirted the mixture of water and condiment into the offended Louis, inducing vomiting to make sure no poisoning would occur. Covered in fur, ink, vomit, and watery mustard, the girl entered the kitchen with her upset canine companion.

A very odd scuttling sound came from the living room so Petra cautiously turned the corner scared as to what she might find. Seated on the coffee table was Honey with a rather odd wriggling thing out of the side of her mouth messing up her whiskers. Slowly stepping toward the cat, Petra cocked her head and squinted trying to discern what the object was. Then she recognized the sand-colored scaly tail as what might very well be the remnants of Phineas the bearded dragon. "HONEY! Tell me you did NOT devour the lizard," Petra shrieked and pulled the jowls of the Persian open to rescue a very damp kitty-spit-lathered Phineas.

The shaking girl brought the limp reptile to the dining room table and placed him on a cloth napkin. Crying softly, Petra wiped the body down and rubbed the little one's chest hoping the poor infant lizard had not died. The eyes flickered and Phineas's tail twitched. "Phinny!" Petra exclaimed and wrapped the bearded dragon up tight in his napkin, gently massaging warmth back in him. She quickly deposited Phineas back into the terrarium on his little sling bed. The lizard curled up under the heat lamp and regarded his rescue maiden with a wary look behind her. "It's okay, Phinny, I promise you I won't let your feline sister beat you up again," Petra wheedled with her hands wringing themselves together.

The poor pet sitter began to sit down on the sofa for a second when a tearing sound from upstairs echoed off the stairway walls. Tentatively, Petra made her way up the stairs and found the should-have-been-closed door to the guest bedroom ajar. She walked inside and was struck in awe at the beautiful damask curtains and silk duvet on the bed. The color scheme was a very beautiful aquamarine with chocolate brown trim.

There at the foot of the bed was Sugar the Himalayan whose eye matched the room décor. She was stretching herself out and scratching down the length of the very expensive drapery. Along the elegant stretch of aquamarine glistening material were long lines of shot silk was down about four inches of the curtains ending at the claw extended paws of a naughty kitty.

"SUGAR!" Petra picked up the Himalayan, tucking the cat close to her body and exited the room, shutting the door behind her tightly. The human and loudly objecting cat came down stairs to the rest of the menagerie. All of which were passed out on respective sections of the couch.

After plopping the cat on the pillows of the nearby sofa, Petra sighed and looked at all her charges. "You are all naughty animals! No dinner for anyone!" As if this chastisement made a dent in the minds of those wagging tails of the dogs or the chuffing of the cats.

Unceremoniously, Petra dragged the dogs down the stairs and crated them without a word or biscuit treat. The girl went up the stairs and cleaned up the now cleared air kitchen and shut the back door. Finally done with her evening, Petra got ready for retirement and settled in her bed only twelve feet away from the crate of now snoring dogs. The cats nestled in the comforter on either side of her as she turned the night table lamp off.

A few minutes later, Petra heard a rather monstrous breaking of wind from the dog crate and Louis whimpering in his sleep. "What was that?" the girl asked her feline bedmates in genuine puzzlement. The rather odiferous aftermath of the fateful inky dinner wafted its way to the bed where the human and cats made gagging noises. "Louis, you just had to have the last word." Petra laughed out loud and buried her nose in a nearby pillow. Such an eloquent ending to a rather adventuresome evening of a pet caretaker.

Feline Doppler Effect

Missy tried her borrowed key in the lock of her friend's door. Dusk was upon her outside, and she really wanted to get inside quickly. Golden-tinged hair fell in her face, and Missy sighed as she pushed it out of her eyes in frustration. Finally in the house, the blonde locked the door behind her and started to look around for the cat. Missy was looking in on her gal pal Helen's beloved feline daughter while she and her husband Steve were on vacation.

"Sneakers!" the girl called out, hearing her voice echo within the walls rather eerily at the late hour. Missy went to all the usual hiding spots the cat had, including a basket where clean towels were kept in the corner of the master bedroom. No furry daughter to be found. Rather distressed, the young woman discovered that workmen who were constructing an addition to the house had left the duct work covers off. "Princess?" Missy called down a duct nervously. A very faint mewing was heard and that got the blonde very upset. The cat was inside the bowels of the house somewhere in the heating and air-conditioning tubes.

An hour passed with Missy sliding along the floors on her belly trying to detect where exactly Sneakers was stuck. She walked all through the house and even the basement calling out for the cat. Defeated, Missy dialed Helen's cell phone number. "Helen? It's Missy. I hate to tell you this, but Sneakers is stuck in the ventilation system."

"Gosh! Is she making any noise? Yes? Okay. The workers told me they had left the vents open and the crawl space beneath the sunroom all day. Maybe Sneakers followed them into a dark part of the house. Go next door to the big house with the porch and ask Rita if you can enlist in her husband Rick's help. Tell her you are my friend and I am out of town, but you need male heft to pry open some portions of the house that are screwed on tight or painted shut. If you cannot get Sneakers out tonight, you can try again tomorrow. Call me again in the morning and let me know what happens. I am sure the cat will be just fine overnight." Helen sighed and hung up on an ashamed, frantic friend entrusted with the welfare of a precious cat.

Running next door, Missy went to enlist the help of a neighbor. A wary dark-haired woman answered her door and gave a quizzical expression at this strange blonde on her porch. "Rita?" Missy smiled, and when she got a slow nod, she went on, "I am Missy a friend of Helen and Steve's, your next-door neighbor. Helen told me I could come by and ask for your help if I needed it while I was taking care of Sneakers, their cat. Well I could really use some assistance in getting Sneakers out of the ventilation system. The construction guys seemed to have left the duct system openings without a cover and the cat fell in. Could you loan me your husband Rick?" Rita laughed and nodded and got her husband to follow me to the house.

Rick was a slightly balding redhead with an easy smile. "So the kitty gave you some trouble, huh?" Missy grinned sheepishly and showed the nice man where she last heard Sneakers. "Oh, I think she is in the crawl space under the sunroom addition," Rick deduced after a few minutes of following the noise of the trapped cat with his ear to the wooden floorboards. Both Rick and Missy went outside with flashlights and sure enough found Sneaker's bright eyes looking at them from behind the grate. The neighbor went back to his house and got some tools. After about thirty minutes of trying to pry the frame of the screen off by flashlight, Rick stood up and squinted into the night darkness. "I think we are going to have to leave the cat there until morning when we have better light to get her out." Missy hung her head and agreed. The man went back to his wife, and Missy locked up the house to return to her home.

The next morning as soon as she could, Missy returned to Helen's place in pursuit of the trapped Sneakers. After calling out the cat's name, the blonde followed the pitiful cries to the crawl space. Missy tapped the board between the crawl space and basement from which she heard a frantic scratching and high-pitched mews. "Sneakers, is that you?" the concerned blonde inquired. After the outraged feline assured the stupid human it was indeed her, Missy scurried around the basement trying to find a screwdriver. Steve had a workbench set up in the basement with a variety of tools in boxes and dangling off hooks. Missy honed in on an orange box she had seen the man of the house use before, and she opened it to find the desired object. Running over to the board, she crooned to the distressed cat, "Sneakers, I am going to get you out really soon." A rather loud meow replied.

Working quickly, Missy removed the screws that had the wood board in place. She had about two more to go when the impatient feline began to throw all the furry heft possible against the panel. Suddenly, Missy found herself flat on her back with the board on her chest and Sneakers on top with her tail held high. "Hello, sweetheart." The squished human smiled up at the cat who glared down. Sneakers let out a domestic lioness roar before bouncing off the panel and running up the stairs to the main level of the house. Missy listened as the cat ran about the length of the home calling out for her parents.

The cell phone vibrated in the blonde's jeans back pocket, and with some groaning, she retrieved it and saw Helen's name on the screen. Carefully placing the phone to her ear, Missy answered, "Helen? Yes, I found Sneakers. The darling was walled back in the crawl space. I unscrewed the board and out she came. You want to talk to Sneakers? Alright." The girl, still on her back, held the phone up in the air as the cat came running down the stairs, made a lap around the basement, raced up the stairs, and did a victory lap upstairs all the while yowling with gusto. Missy smiled and talked to Helen, "Did you hear that fine example of the feline Doppler effect? Yes, the princess is just fine. See you in a few days."

Dropping her head back down, the girl began to laugh hysterically as she listened to Sneakers doing a fine roadrunner imitation. Missy never thought she would ever hear the actual demonstration of the Doppler effect by a cat.

Possum Race

Emily sighed as she turned the corner to the house of Addie, her canine ward, to find naughtiness going down. That pup was burying something into another hole in her backyard and even worse it seemed to be a chewed on lamb shank bone with decayed flesh still attached. "Bad girl!" Emily snatched the offensive stolen meal away and promptly ditched it in a city-provided garbage can. Undoubtedly, one long night lay ahead given Addie's stomach problems.

Sure enough, a rumble coming from the dog's abdomen signaled issues around six thirty that evening. Addie immediately vomited water and soggy kibble onto Emily's feet. "Eeewww! You are going to get a good bath for this one, young lady!" She dragged her ward into the shower with her for sanitary reasons as well as punishment. Once both of them were cleaned up, they went on a walk to feel better. After all, fresh air always lifts one's mood.

At the park, Emily came across Gina, a neighbor, with her own dog.. "Have you heard about the deranged possum around these parts? A fat gray one has been attacking people and pups. No reason either. Climbs out of the sewer to take his pound of flesh for fun. So far that sick rodent has gone after humans for three consecutive nights. Watch out tonight!" she warned. Just what Emily needed on top of a sick canine ward—pissed off marsupial. Good thing that Addie had Staffordshire terrier in her.

Emily explained to her client Mandy over the phone what clandestine snack was eaten and received advice on how to proceed. "Damn it! I swear that dog has a bottomless pit for her stomach. Look, you must give her lots of water and take her on long walks whenever she asks for a potty break. Not just letting her use the backyard. A walk will stretch out her tummy muscles, which encourages needed bowel evacuation. Addie is no spring chicken and her stomach cannot handle heavy meat much less rotten lamb. If there isn't any improvement in three days, then you need the veterinary doctor to examine her. Have fun!" she spoke with empathy and frustration in her voice.

Like clockwork, Addie required hourly walks to flush ill-gotten noms. Naturally, it was a windy, cold, moonless night. At three in the morning, Emily bundled up for another neighborhood park trip. "Let's keep you warm, girl!" She placed a warm red sweater on Addie whose tail wagged furiously. Emily thought to herself how she deserved extra financial compensation for this job as she walked her canine ward.

When the pair arrived at their destination, shadows, wind, and crunchy leaves amped up creepy vibes. Addie managed to pass another shot of dark liquid from her rear end in that cold night breeze. On their way back home, both hear scrambling noises behind them. Lo and behold, a grayish form climbed out from the sewer right beneath the park's corner curb.

Emily gasped when she saw streetlight glint off some impressive fangs inside that possum's mouth. When that creature of sewer life lunged at the stunned pair, they froze in horror. Addie's fight or flight switched on, and she took off for home with her caretaker close behind. "Run, girl, run!" Emily hollered as they sped down the sidewalk. She could not believe how fast both her canine ward and her own body could move when needed. After the three of them had run half a block, that possum gave up chasing his targets for easier victims.

Adrenaline compelled human and dog to sprint until they reached home. Emily scrambled with her keys out of pure panic. She finally let them both inside and held on to her canine ward in relief. "Thank goodness we made it, girl." Addie got some water while her caretaker followed suit. Exhausted, the pair fell into bed together for some much-needed sleep.

That following morning, Emily called her client to tell her tale. Rather than sympathy, ridicule was given. "The animal probably only charged out of self-defense. No life could have ever been in danger. You just got spooked, silly girl!" Mandy laughed. Emily grumbled under her breath. Maybe her client was right. Oh well. At least she and Addie won the possum race.

About the Author

The author is a woman in her mid-forties who has to start over again. Her past holds reminders of happiness's existence. Like J. M. Barrie once said, "God gave us memories so we may have roses in December." The author now tries to create mental fertilizer in the present moment for a future crop of blissful emotional flowers.

CPSIA information can be obtained
at www.ICGtesting.com
Printed in the USA
LVHW071808171222
735440LV00035B/610